Birth of the Republic

─── **Alden R. Carter** ───

★ # BIRTH OF THE REPUBLIC ★

Franklin Watts
New York/London/Toronto
Sydney/1988
A First Book

9325231   +
5/89 11⁹⁵   973.3
            C 24

Library of Congress Cataloging-in-Publication Data

Carter, Alden R.
Birth of the republic / Alden R. Carter.
p.   cm. — (A First book)
Bibliography: p.
Includes index.
Summary: Discusses the final campaigns of the Revolutionary War
and the structuring of a new nation, from the formulation of the
Articles of Confederation to the adoption of the Constitution.
ISBN 0-531-10572-5
1. United States—History—Revolution, 1775–1783—Campaigns—
Juvenile literature.   2. United States—History—Revolution,
1775–1783—Peace—Juvenile literature.   3. United States—History—
Confederation, 1783–1789—Juvenile literature.   [1. United States—
History—Revolution, 1775–1783—Campaigns.   2. United States—
History—Confederation, 1783–1789.]   I. Title.   II. Series.
E230.C335   1988
973.3—dc19   88-5622   CIP   AC

For two friends of much good advice:
Dean Markwardt and John Bittrich

Other Books by Alden R. Carter

NONFICTION

Supercomputers (with Wayne J. LeBlanc)
Modern China
Modern Electronics (with Wayne J. LeBlanc)
Radio: From Marconi to the Space Age
Illinois
Colonies in Revolt
Darkest Hours
At the Forge of Liberty

FICTION

Growing Season
Wart, Son of Toad
Sheila's Dying

Contents

Chapter 1
Looking for a Fight
13

Chapter 2
The Lion at Bay
20

Chapter 3
Making Peace
31

Chapter 4
Confederation of Free States
47

Chapter 5
The Constitutional Convention
58

Chapter 6
"We the People. . ."
78

Epilogue
Building the Nation
89

Suggested Reading 91

Index 92

Many thanks to all who helped with *Birth of the Republic,* particularly my editor, Marjory Kline; my mother, Hilda Carter Fletcher; and my friends Don Beyer, Sue Babcock, and Georgette Frazer. As always, my wife, Carol, deserves much of the credit.

★ 1 ★

Looking for a Fight

At the crest of a low hill, the two generals reined in their horses for a last look at the city's defenses. General George Washington, commander of America's Continental army, glared through the early dusk as if his blue-gray eyes could burn a hole in the British fortifications encircling New York City.

Beside him, General Comte de Rochambeau, commander of the French troops in America, waited patiently. For days the French general had been arguing against an attack: the fortifications were too strong, the American and French troops outnumbered by the British defenders. Yet Washington had stubbornly persisted in trying to find a way to assault the city.

The handsome, heavyset Frenchman understood Washington's frustration. For three restless years, Washington had waited for the main British army to make a move. Reports of fierce fighting in the Carolinas, Virginia, and on the frontier arrived at the commander-in-chief's headquarters. Washington had longed to hurry to one of the Revolution's lesser battlegrounds, but his duty had kept him in the vicinity of New York City. All he could do was send instructions to his generals, dispatch what reinforcements and supplies he could spare, then turn back to the waiting.

Less than three weeks had passed since Rochambeau had led his five thousand French soldiers into the American camp. In the short time since, he felt that he had come to understand Washington surprisingly well. He could see that the tall Virginian was not a patient man by nature. Behind the iron reserve Washington used to cloak his emotions, the man ached for action, for a chance to strike a telling blow in the cause of liberty. But Rochambeau also knew that Washington was not a reckless man. The American army had survived because Washington had learned when to fight, when to run, and when to simply bide his time.

That an American army existed at all on this late July day in 1781 was something of a miracle to Rochambeau. In six years of war, the British had won most of the battles but had somehow failed to crush the spirit of revolution in America. Time and again, the American army had suffered staggering blows on the battlefield, but Washington had always saved it to fight another day. Winter after winter, the army had withered to almost nothing, but Washington had nursed it back to health with each summer. Rochambeau admired Washington's stubborn courage, but it could not make up for a lack of men and guns. Washington must give up the idea of attacking New York, and look elsewhere for the fight he craved.

Washington sighed and shook his head. Talking quietly, the two generals rode back toward camp. They agreed to meet again on the morrow.

How to Use the Army?

For three more weeks, Washington and Rochambeau wrestled with the problem of how best to use their army of some eleven thousand men. To the north, the British posed no active threat between New York City and far-off Canada. In the Deep South, General Nathanael Greene had waged a remarkable campaign to frustrate British plans for retaking the Carolinas and Georgia. The real danger—and opportunity—lay in Virginia, where General Lord Charles Cornwallis and six thousand British troops were playing cat and mouse with the small American army under the Marquis de Lafayette, a gallant French volunteer in the American army.

Much as Washington wanted to help Lafayette, marching south presented a terrible danger. In New York City, General Sir Henry Clinton had some seventeen thousand British and German troops. The British regulars were perhaps the finest infantry in the world, the German mercenaries tough veterans hired to fight in America. If Washington abandoned his blockade of the city, Clinton could seize the Middle Atlantic states almost unopposed, perhaps ending the war. Still, there were also terrible dangers in doing nothing. The long years of war had taken a toll on America. The economy was a shambles, the Continental Congress nearly powerless, and the people weakening in their resolve. Could the Revolution survive another winter?

Washington also had to worry about events far from America's shores. America had become only one of many battlefields in the wider war between Britain and America's European allies, France and Spain. Washington liked and trusted Rochambeau, but the French general took orders from distant Paris. If the British won a decisive victory in Europe, the Caribbean, or India, the French might make peace. Even if the American army made it through another winter, it might face the next summer's campaign without the vital aid of the French army and navy. The possibility gnawed at Washington. Perhaps the time had come to risk everything for a great victory.

The British Strategy

In New York City, General Clinton was happy to wait for the Revolution to collapse. He had seen that battlefield victories had little lasting value in this huge land. At one time or another in the war, the British had occupied nearly every major city along the seacoast. America had simply shrugged off the losses and gone on fighting. Yet Clinton believed that the Americans would eventually realize that they could not defeat the great might of the British army and navy. Sooner or later, the Americans would accept Britain's generous surrender terms. A few hit-and-run raids would keep pressure on the Americans while Clinton waited and Washington steamed.

Clinton's strategy maddened his second-in-command. Lord Cornwallis believed in attacking the rebels wherever they showed their faces. If they refused to stand and fight, then destroy their crops, storehouses, and—if necessary—their homes. Cornwallis blamed Clinton for not sending him enough troops and supplies for a successful campaign in the Carolinas and Georgia. Deeply frustrated, Cornwallis had marched north into Virginia in the spring of 1781. If he could break the spirit of the largest and richest colony, perhaps the rest of America would give up.

The Virginia Raids

Fighting was already underway in Virginia. Several months before, Clinton had sent the American traitor Benedict Arnold to raid along the James River. Arnold was a brilliant soldier. Earlier in the war, he had won spectacular victories as an American general, but Congress had promoted less talented men over his head. A bitter Arnold had offered to betray the important American post at West Point, New York, to the British. American cavalry had intercepted a British officer acting as a go-between. News that the plot had been discovered reached Arnold in time for him to escape to New York City. As payment for his services, he had received the rank of brigadier general in the British army.

Cornwallis arrived to take command in late May 1781. Soon after, Arnold was recalled to New York City. Cornwallis increased the size of the raids, capturing Richmond and pushing as far west as Charlottesville, where his cavalry nearly captured Governor Thomas Jefferson.

Badly outnumbered, Lafayette could not risk a major battle with Cornwallis. But the twenty-three-year-old Frenchman was a skillful general. He dodged Cornwallis's blows and struck whenever he could at exposed British detachments. By mid-June, Cornwallis had tired of the game. He marched his army toward the shores of Chesapeake Bay, where he could rest his men and coordinate future operations with Clinton.

At Williamsburg, Cornwallis received letters from Clinton. Cornwallis was to establish a strong naval base on the Chesapeake and prepare to send half his troops back to New York. The defensive orders disgusted Cornwallis, but he set about obeying them. He selected Yorktown as the best site for the base and began constructing fortifications. Lafayette established his own lines at a safe distance.

The Admiral's Letter

At the allied camp outside New York City, Washington and Rochambeau had news of Cornwallis's move to Yorktown. It did not resolve their problem. Even if they left the Middle Atlantic

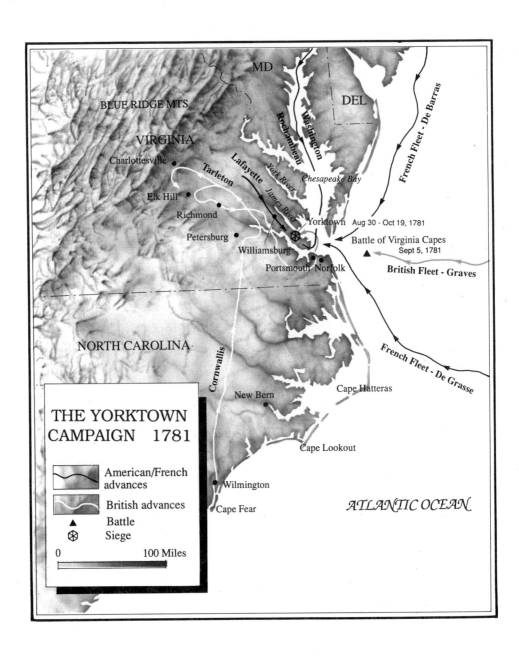

MD

DEL

BLUE RIDGE MTS

VIRGINIA

Charlottesville

French Fleet - De Barras

Rochambeau

Washington

Tarleton

Lafayette

York River

Chesapeake Bay

Elk Hill

James River

Richmond

Yorktown   Aug 30 - Oct 19, 1781

Petersburg

Battle of Virginia Capes
Sept 5, 1781

Williamsburg

Portsmouth Norfolk

British Fleet - Graves

NORTH CAROLINA

Cornwallis

French Fleet - De Grasse

New Bern

Cape Hatteras

Cape Lookout

THE YORKTOWN
CAMPAIGN   1781

Wilmington

Cape Fear

ATLANTIC OCEAN

American/French
advances

British advances

▲   Battle

⊛   Siege

0   100 Miles

states unprotected to march into Virginia, it was doubtful that they could defeat Cornwallis. The Royal Navy controlled the sea and could bring reinforcements to Yorktown at will.

On August 14, a letter arrived that changed the entire situation. Admiral Comte de Grasse, commander of the French West Indies fleet, wrote that he intended to sail to Chesapeake Bay, arriving at the end of August and departing in mid-October. In the intervening weeks, he could provide the help of his warships, three thousand soldiers, and a large number of cannon.

The letter abruptly ended the debate over strategy. Washington saw clearly what he should do. The army would march south as quickly as possible to join Lafayette outside Yorktown. If de Grasse could cut off the sea approaches to Yorktown, they would have Cornwallis and his army of six thousand trapped. Rochambeau readily agreed to the bold plan.

Washington could agonize for weeks over a decision, then act with great speed once he had made up his mind. As he planned the complicated move south, his mastery of military detail had never been more obvious. He wrote de Grasse, asking for transport ships to meet the army at the head of Chesapeake Bay. He sent orders to Lafayette, instructing him to cut off Cornwallis's escape route into North Carolina. He placed General William Heath in charge of a small American force remaining behind to watch Clinton.

On August 21, 1781, the American and French troops began the march south toward Yorktown and an extraordinary moment in history.

★ 2 ★

The Lion at Bay

The British called Washington "the fox," a grudging compliment to his cunning. He had a trick ready to disguise the army's move south. He ordered the construction of an elaborate camp in New Jersey. Clinton heard of the activity and concluded that Washington planned to use the camp as a base for attacking Staten Island, across the harbor from New York City.

Washington's army occupied the camp for only a day or two before slipping away. The columns crossed the Delaware River at Trenton and, safe from pursuit, marched through Philadelphia on September 2, flags flying and drums beating. Clinton had already begun to suspect a trick, and news of the parade confirmed his worst fears—a huge trap was closing on Cornwallis. A more aggressive general than Clinton might have struck up the Hudson River, in the hope that Washington would rush back to defend the Middle Atlantic colonies. Clinton, however, decided to depend on the Royal Navy to rescue Cornwallis.

Fleets on the Move

On the march, Washington and Rochambeau agonized about events beyond the seaward horizon. Everything now depended on the French navy. Admiral de Grasse was bound for Chesapeake Bay to cut off Cornwallis from escape or reinforcement. Admiral Comte de Barras was sailing south from Newport with a smaller French squadron, carrying supplies and heavy guns for the siege of Yorktown. Somewhere in between, the powerful British fleet was maneuvering, still ignorant of the allied plan.

The British commander, Admiral Thomas Graves, knew that de Grasse and de Barras were at sea. He hoped to destroy de Barras before the French squadrons could unite. If he had known of Washington's plan, he might have made for Chesapeake Bay without delay, but instead he wasted days sweeping the ocean for de Barras. Finally, he turned south to "look in" on the Chesapeake.

On September 4, Rochambeau rode into the American camp to find the usually restrained Washington "waving his hat at me with . . . the greatest joy." De Grasse had arrived at the Chesapeake; Cornwallis was trapped.

The Battle of the Virginia Capes

The French West Indies fleet of twenty-four mighty ships of the line (the battleships of the day) had reached Chesapeake Bay on August 26. The flag of Admiral de Grasse flew from the 110-gun *Ville de Paris,* the most powerful warship in the world. De Grasse sent four of his ships of the line to blockade Yorktown. On September 5, he ordered his three thousand infantrymen ashore to join Lafayette. The unloading was nearly complete when lookouts spotted tall masts to the southeast. The British fleet had arrived.

De Grasse ordered his ships to sea at once. The crews executed his orders so quickly that two thousand sailors ashore, gathering supplies, could only stare dumbfounded as sails unfurled and their ships turned toward the mouth of the bay and the battle of the Virginia Capes. The French had the advantage. De Grasse outnumbered Graves by twenty-four to nineteen in ships of the line, seventeen hundred to fourteen hundred in cannon, and seventeen thousand to fourteen thousand in men. But the renowned seamen of Britain had won against far greater odds in the past.

Outside the bay, the French ships formed into a long line on a southeasterly course. The British fleet turned to take a parallel course. Slowly, the long battle lines drew together. At 4:00 P.M. the fleets opened fire. For two hours the great ships blasted away at each other. Often ships were so close that sailors could see the faces of the men on the decks opposite through the fire and smoke.

As dusk fell, the fleets drew apart. Through the night, the crews labored to repair the damage of battle. The living wrapped the dead in sailcloth and sent the bodies to "watery graves." Surgeons treated the wounded. Ships carpenters did their best to repair damaged rigging and leaking hulls. The French had come out of the battle with a slight edge. Their heavier fire had severely damaged five British ships, one so badly that it had to be abandoned. The British had suffered 336 dead and wounded to 209 on the French side.

For three days, the fleets sailed slowly southeast, each side watching for the other to make a mistake. On September 9, de Barras's squadron was sighted to the north, making for the

At the battle of the Virginia Capes in September 1781, the French fleet succeeded in blocking British ships from reinforcing Cornwallis's embattled troops at Yorktown.

Chesapeake. The arrival of de Barras added eight ships of the line to the French fleet. Graves admitted defeat and steered for New York that night, leaving Cornwallis to his fate.

De Grasse sent transports up the Chesapeake to pick up Washington's army. By September 26, all of Washington and Rochambeau's troops were ashore at Williamsburg. The spirits of the troops soared as they joined Lafayette's men in the lines before Yorktown. Nearly everyone felt that a great victory lay ahead.

Caught in the Trap

Inside Yorktown, Cornwallis knew his situation was becoming desperate. A dribble of reinforcements had increased his army to some eighty-four hundred men, but Washington had nearly twice that number. Even worse, the army surrounding Yorktown was composed not of raw militia but of seasoned American and French troops. Cornwallis pulled in his outposts and prepared to withstand a siege. If he could hold out long enough, perhaps the British navy might yet win through to rescue him by sea.

Yorktown occupied a low bluff on the north side of a narrow peninsula between the York and James rivers. The town's sixty houses and several public buildings overlooked the broad York River. On the far side of the York, a little more than half a mile from Yorktown, lay Gloucester Point. It was occupied by a small British force under Colonel Banastre Tarleton. Batteries of cannon on the north and south shores, as well as two Royal Navy frigates in the river, protected the British camps from attack by water.

On the landward side of Yorktown, the British had erected a circle of strong earthen walls, called ramparts. Several earthen fortresses, called redoubts, stood in the fields beyond. On September 30, Cornwallis ordered all but the two strongest redoubts on the southeast and one on the north evacuated.

The Siege Begins

The allies quickly occupied the abandoned British redoubts. Under fire from the British lines, the Americans enlarged the redoubts and began mounting cannon to fire on the town. Behind the allied lines, supply parties gathered every shovel, pick, hatchet, and axe they could find. Baron von Steuben, the experienced German officer on Washington's staff, directed the construction of large wicker baskets. Filled with earth, they would form nearly cannon-proof ramparts. Men wrestled heavy siege cannon the six miles overland from the landing site on the James.

The lay of the land made the southeast end of the town the most vulnerable to attack. Washington decided to dig a long trench called a parallel 600 yards from the British defenses. His men would mount cannon in the first parallel, then push zigzag trenches, called approaches, toward the British lines. At 300 yards, they would begin a second parallel. If cannon fire from the second parallel did not force the British to surrender, then a third parallel would be dug even closer to the defenses. Infantry would charge the town from this final parallel.

On the night of October 6, fifteen hundred Americans began digging the first parallel while another twenty-five hundred stood guard. Even the British had to admit that no troops could dig like the Americans. By morning, the parallel was deep enough to protect the diggers from the constant fire from the town. The Americans lengthened the parallel and built redoubts and protected batteries for their cannon.

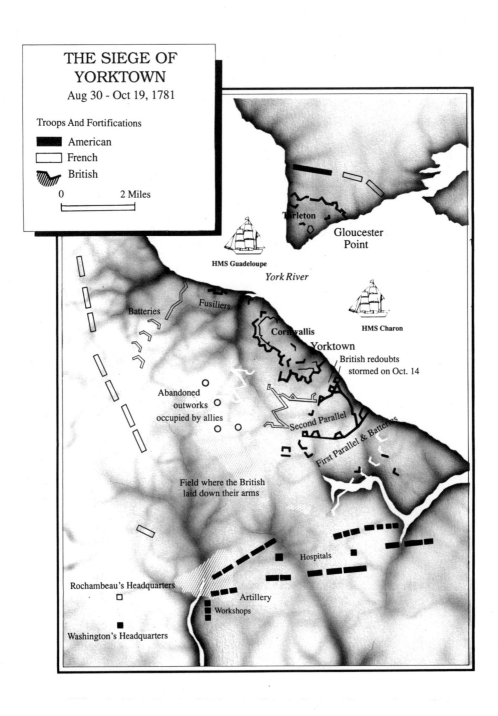

THE SIEGE OF
YORKTOWN
Aug 30 - Oct 19, 1781

Troops And Fortifications
  American
  French
  British

0   2 Miles

Tarleton

Gloucester
Point

HMS Guadeloupe

York River

HMS Charon

Batteries

Fusiliers

Cornwallis

Yorktown

British redoubts
stormed on Oct. 14

Abandoned
outworks
occupied by allies

Second Parallel

First Parallel & Batteries

Field where the British
laid down their arms

Hospitals

Rochambeau's Headquarters

Artillery
Workshops

Washington's Headquarters

The allied cannon opened fire from the first parallel October 9. Three days of furious bombardment silenced most of the British guns, destroyed one frigate, and drove the other ship away. All the while, the digging continued. The first parallel was lengthened to 2,000 yards and the zigzag approaches pushed toward the British lines. On the night of October 11, the Americans started digging the second parallel, 300 yards closer to the town.

Night Attack

The two British redoubts near the York blocked the completion of the second parallel. Washington planned a night attack. The French would assault the redoubt nearest the end of the parallel and the Americans the redoubt on the riverbank. The two attacking forces slipped from the allied trenches shortly after dark on the evening of October 14.

Colonel Alexander Hamilton led an elite force of four hundred American light infantry. The men moved stealthily, their guns unloaded to prevent accidental firing. They reached the redoubt unchallenged and swarmed over the rampart. Ten minutes of bloody hand-to-hand fighting left the redoubt in American hands.

The French had a harder time. Discovered when still 350 yards from their objective, they attacked under heavy fire. The French were seasoned professionals; they took their losses and pushed ahead. After a terrible half hour of fighting, the defenders threw down their weapons and begged for mercy.

The victories in the night proved decisive. By morning, the army's tireless diggers had extended the second parallel to include the captured redoubts. Cornwallis knew the end was near. He wrote Clinton: "My situation now becomes very critical. We

dare not show a gun to their old batteries, and I expect that their new ones will open [fire] tomorrow morning. . . . The safety of [Yorktown] is, therefore, so precarious that I cannot recommend that [you] run great risk in endeavouring to save us."

Proud Cornwallis hated the prospect of presiding over one of the greatest defeats in the history of his nation. He planned a final, desperate tactic. He would ferry his army across to Tarleton's camp on Gloucester Point, smash through the allied lines, and flee overland to New York City. The British began loading their boats shortly before midnight on October 16. Only a fraction of his troops made it across before a violent storm came howling in from the Atlantic, forcing the boats back to shore and ending Cornwallis's forlorn hope of escape.

The Final Bombardment

On the morning of October 17, the allies opened up with all their guns. The British fortifications came tumbling down under the battering. The once-proud redcoats huddled in the dust and smoke. Cornwallis could avoid the inevitable no longer.

At 10:00 A.M., there was a brief lull in the firing as the allies shifted their guns to new targets. Suddenly, a shout went up from the French end of the line. On the ramparts opposite, a

General Washington and
General Comte de Rochambeau,
commander of the French troops
in America, give final orders
as the siege of Yorktown
is about to begin.

drummer was beating the call for a truce. Orders passed down the line and the last guns ceased firing. A British officer carrying a white handkerchief emerged from the ruined fortifications.

Washington was writing letters when an aide burst in with a letter from the British commander. It read, in part: "I propose a cessation of hostilities . . . to settle terms for the surrender of the posts of York and Gloucester. I have the honor to be Sir Your most obedient and most humble Servant, Cornwallis."

The World Turned Upside Down

Legend says that a British band played an old song, *The World Turned Upside Down,* as the garrison marched out of Yorktown to surrender at noon on October 19, 1781. A total of 8,087 British soldiers and sailors laid down their weapons. Another 156 had died in the siege. The allies' losses were only 72 killed and 190 wounded. Yet they had won a continent.

★ 3 ★

———————— Making Peace ————————

News of Cornwallis's surrender spread through the thirteen colonies as fast as riders could carry it. Patriots rejoiced with parades, bonfires, and church services of thanksgiving. Most people expected more battles, but final victory seemed at last in reach.

According to a witness, the British prime minister, Lord Frederick North, took the news of Yorktown "as he would have taken a [musket] ball in his breast." He cried, "Oh God! It is all over."

Negotiations

A shocked and angered King George III remained determined to carry on the war, but Parliament, the British legislature, had seen enough. Parliament voted to begin peace negotiations. The king reluctantly agreed. The Continental Congress responded by naming John Adams, John Jay, Benjamin Franklin, and Henry

Laurens to represent America's interests at the peace talks in Paris.

Preliminary talks on a host of difficult issues began in April 1782. The task of the American peace commission was complicated by the interests of America's allies, France and Spain. The three allies had agreed not to make peace without first agreeing among themselves—and France was in no hurry to end a war that was going well.

The negotiations dragged on through the summer of 1782. In America, Washington's army resumed its watch outside New York City. In the South, where the British still held Charleston and Savannah, occasional sharp skirmishes were fought. And, as always, the frontier was restless.

The Fate of the Loyalists

The British peace commission sought to protect the rights and property of Americans who had remained loyal to the king. Although a sizable majority of Americans had eventually come to favor independence, perhaps twenty percent of the population—some five hundred thousand people—were Loyalists.

As the war wound down, most Loyalists gave up the king's cause and faded into the general population. However, some eighty thousand Loyalists chose to leave America rather than seek peace with their neighbors and the new future. About fifty thousand settled in the Maritime provinces of Canada and another ten thousand in Ontario. A few moved to the West Indies, and the rest found new homes in Britain. Eventually, some returned to the United States.

The American peace commission agreed to a treaty that would pay the Loyalists for lost property, but the promise went largely unkept for many years.

In his eighteenth-century painting, Benjamin West depicts the American delegation to the Paris peace talks in 1783. From left to right: John Jay, John Adams, Benjamin Franklin, Henry Laurens, and William Temple Franklin, secretary to the American delegation. The members of the British delegation, who were to appear on the right, refused to sit for their portraits, and the painting was never finished.

Fixing the Borders

Drawing the boundaries of the new nation posed a devilishly complex problem. Britain was determined to keep Canada, northern Maine, Florida, and as much of the Great Lakes region as possible. Spain not only held firm title to the lands west of the Mississippi, but also claimed considerable land to the east. France supported the Spanish claims in hope of receiving disputed territory in Europe and the West Indies.

It became obvious that negotiations could drag on for years if all four nations kept suggesting different boundaries. The British and American commissioners agreed to a secret treaty. The southern border of the United States would extend from the Atlantic to the Mississippi on a line roughly parallel to what is today the northern border of Florida. (Britain later gave Florida to Spain as part of the final treaty.) The western border was set at the Mississippi River with New Orleans and the delta region remaining in Spanish hands.

After much discussion, the commissioners agreed on a northeast border between the United States and Canada. However, their maps were poor, and years of dispute would follow before the final lines were settled in 1818.

Dividing the Great Lakes region presented still more problems. This vast wilderness had been the scene of a little-known

Many colonists who had remained loyal to Britain would suffer harsh fates. Here Loyalist outcasts camp by the St. Lawrence River, on their way to new homes in Canada.

chapter in the war. In Paris, the commissioners argued about the significance of campaigns fought far from civilization. Little attention was paid to the rights of the people who knew the land best—the Indians.

The Six Nations

Before the Revolution, white settlement had pushed beyond the Appalachians into the western reaches of today's New York and Pennsylvania. This was the land of the Iroquois Confederation, or the Six Nations. The Iroquois were a mighty people, feared by other Indian tribes living as far west as the Mississippi.

The Iroquois had adopted many features of European civilization. Most of the Iroquois lived in permanent settlements of log or frame houses. Although they still depended on hunting and fishing, they also tended cornfields, vegetable gardens, and apple, pear, and peach orchards. The Six Nations had a written constitution and an organized government. A fair number of the people had become Christians and could read and write.

Not long after the Revolution began, fighting spread to the frontier. Loyalists, sometimes aided by British officers and regular troops from Canada, fought patriots for control of the white settlements. At first, the Iroquois remained aloof from what they viewed as a family quarrel. Soon British agents and representatives of the Continental Congress arrived with gifts, promises, and requests for help. The British, the Iroquois' old allies from the time of the French and Indian wars, had the better arguments. The British had tried to prevent the spread of white settlement and promised to guarantee the safety of Indian lands in the future. Four of the Iroquois tribes—the Mohawks, Onondagas, Cayugas, and Senecas—agreed to fight for the British.

Joseph Brant, a Mohawk Indian chief, was widely feared by colonists who lived along the New York and Pennsylvania frontiers.

The two remaining—the Oneidas and the Tuscaroras—chose the patriot side.

Soon the frontier was ablaze. In the summer of 1778, a force of Loyalists and Senecas stormed through the Wyoming Valley of Pennsylvania, burning some one thousand houses including the entire town of Wilkes-Barre. At Wintermoot, they nearly wiped out the defending militia force, killing 227 and capturing perhaps 50 others. Only about 60 militiamen escaped.

In the Mohawk Valley of New York, the Iroquois were led by a remarkable man, Joseph Brant, whose Indian name was Thayendanegea. A full-blooded Mohawk, Brant had received an English education in Connecticut, had visited London, and, in the years before the war, had served as secretary to the British superintendent of Indian affairs in Quebec. Yet his heart had remained thoroughly Indian. He returned to his people and became their war chief. Daring and ingenious, he kept the "Bloody Mohawk" in a state of alarm for years.

Sullivan's Expedition

The frontier settlers bombarded the Continental Congress and General Washington with pleas for help. Washington responded by ordering General John Sullivan and thirty-seven hundred troops to the frontier in the summer of 1779. Like most whites of his day, Washington had little respect for Indians. He gave Sullivan harsh orders: "[pursue] total destruction of [the Iroquois] settlements and the capture of as many prisoners of every age and sex as possible."

Sullivan carried out the destruction with a vengeance. He reported burning forty Indian towns—some with over one hundred houses—and destroying their fields, orchards, and livestock. With winter not far away, the Indians lost some 160,000

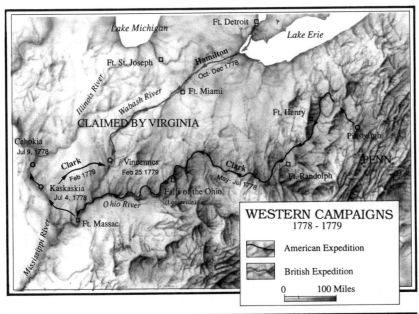

Lake Michigan

Ft. Detroit

Lake Erie

Ft. St. Joseph

Hamilton
Oct- Dec 1778

Ft. Miami

Illinois River

Wabash River

Ft. Henry

CLAIMED BY VIRGINIA

Pittsburgh

Cahokia
Jul 9, 1778

Clark
Feb 1779

Vincennes
Feb 25 1779

Clark
May- Jul 1778

PENN.

Kaskaskia
Jul 4, 1778

Ohio River

Falls of the Ohio
(Louisville)

Ft. Randolph

Mississippi River

Ft. Massac

WESTERN CAMPAIGNS
1778 - 1779

American Expedition

British Expedition

0   100 Miles

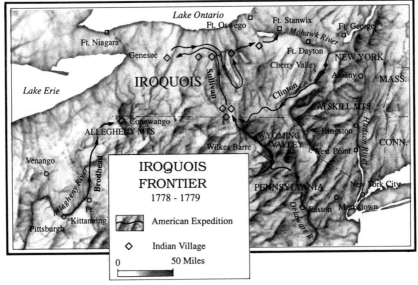

Lake Ontario

Ft. Stanwix

Ft. Oswego

Ft. George

Ft. Niagara

Mohawk River

Genesee

Ft. Dayton

NEW YORK

Sullivan

Cherry Valley

IROQUOIS

Albany

MASS.

Lake Erie

Clinton

CATSKILL MTS.

Conewango

ALLEGHENY MTS

Kingston

Hudson River

CONN.

Venango

Wilkes Barre

WYOMING
VALLEY

West Point

Allegheny River

Brodhead

PENNSYLVANIA

New York City

Ft.
Kittanning

Easton

Morristown

Pittsburgh

Delaware R.

IROQUOIS
FRONTIER
1778 - 1779

American Expedition

◇   Indian Village

0   50 Miles

bushels of corn to the invader's torch. Although Sullivan had disregarded the second half of his orders and brought back no hostages to insure the good behavior of the tribes, Congress voted him its thanks. That same summer, an expedition from Pittsburgh devastated the Indian villages along the Allegheny River.

In fury, the Indians struck back, attacking frontier villages and isolated homesteads again and again. However, the power of the Six Nations had been broken. At the end of the war, their lands would go to white settlers. The accomplishments of a proud and brave people faded into history.

Wilderness War

West of the Iroquois lands lay a great wilderness. Pittsburgh, at the head of the Ohio River, was the last American settlement of any size. Below the Ohio, Daniel Boone and other brave pioneers had established outposts in what is today Kentucky. To the north and west, the British held the old French town of Vincennes on the Wabash River, the small French settlements of Kaskaskia and Cahokia on the Mississippi, and a few scattered forts that were little more than trading posts.

Lieutenant Colonel Henry Hamilton, the British agent at Detroit, served as governor of this vast region. Hamilton stirred up Indian hatred of the American pioneers. He supplied the tribes with rum and weapons, and—at least according to the pioneers—paid a bounty for white prisoners and scalps.

In the early years of the Revolution, the Indians rampaged across the "dark and bloody ground" of northern Kentucky. The pioneers—"the long knives" as the Indians called them—fought back, killing with a brutality equal to that of the Indians. It was a war with no noncombatants on either side; every man, woman, and child knew the fear of the swift, murderous raid.

*Daniel Boone and his followers look upon
the Kentucky wilderness for the first time.*

Reports of the fighting reached the Continental Congress, together with urgent requests for an attack on Detroit and "Hair Buyer" Hamilton. Hard pressed to meet the needs of the war in the East, Congress could supply few men and little equipment. In the spring of 1777 and again in early 1778, small expeditions set out from Pittsburgh, but neither made it more than a few dozen miles before bad weather, lack of supplies, and the Indian danger drove them back.

George Rogers Clark

An impatient young Virginian took matters into his own hands. At twenty-six, George Rogers Clark was an imposing figure: tall, immensely strong, with flaming red hair to match his temperament. An experienced Indian fighter, he was Virginia's military commander in Kentucky.

Clark had a plan to undermine British influence north of the Ohio. He would capture the British outposts at Kaskaskia and Cahokia in the Illinois country, swing back east to take Vincennes, and then—if enough recruits could be found among the French residents of the three towns—strike at Hamilton in Detroit. Patrick Henry, then Virginia's governor, approved Clark's ambitious plan.

In May 1778, Clark set out by boat from Pittsburgh with a tiny force of 150 men. He expected to meet one of his captains and another 200 men at the Falls of the Ohio where Louisville, Kentucky, now stands. Instead, he found fewer than 50 men waiting. At that point, a lesser man might have given up, but not Clark. On June 26, he loaded his "army" onto flatboats and headed down the river.

Nine hundred miles below Pittsburgh, Clark hid his boats at an abandoned outpost, Fort Massac. Between Fort Massac and Kaskaskia on the Mississippi lay 120 miles of trackless wilderness. The men started out in good spirits, but the guide lost his way. He found it again only after Clark threatened to hang him. Food ran out. Insects tormented the troops. Moccasins wore through and some men had to march barefoot.

On July 4, the Americans finally reached Kaskaskia. Hungry and tired, they wasted little time in planning an attack. Clark marched his men through an open gate and directly to the home of the town's commander, an elderly French officer in the British service. Summoned to the door, he took one look at Clark's force and surrendered his small garrison.

Clark informed the French residents of Kaskaskia that France had entered the war on the side of America. Almost all the townspeople agreed to support the cause of independence. Clark dispatched a few men to take possession of Cahokia some forty miles upriver. A French priest, Father Gibault, volunteered to go to Vincennes with a request for the town's surrender. He was successful, and Clark sent one of his captains to take charge of the garrison of local French militia at Vincennes.

So far not a shot had been fired in anger. Clark called for a conference with the Indians. Thousands of chiefs and warriors attended. They took a liking to Clark and made pledges of peace.

Hamilton Strikes

In Detroit, Hamilton received news of Clark's invasion of the king's territory. He quickly gathered a force of five hundred whites and Indians and marched on Vincennes. The French militiamen refused to fight, and the American captain surrendered. Convinced that fighting was over for the season, Hamilton dismissed most of his Indian allies and settled in at Vincennes to wait until spring.

He had underestimated Clark badly. On February 6, 1779, Clark set out for Vincennes with 127 men. The march across

George Rogers Clark and his men advance toward Vincennes and French towns in Illinois in an attempt to counteract the English influence in the Northwest.

the winter wilderness was a nearly indescribable torture. Heavy rains fell, turning creeks into rivers and swamps into lakes. Often the soldiers had to wade chest deep through freezing water. Time and again men stumbled and nearly drowned before being pulled to safety. Food began to run out, game was scarce, and the army's gunpowder was soaked and useless. Somehow, Clark managed to keep the men moving.

On the evening of February 17, the Americans heard the sunset gun fired from Fort Sackville at the center of Vincennes. Clark estimated that they had only nine more miles to cover. But a flooded river forced a detour to the south. It took six more agonizing days to reach dry ground two miles from Vincennes. Scouts picked up a Frenchman from the town. He gave the Americans the discouraging news that Hamilton had a garrison of some one hundred whites and two hundred Indians.

After all the suffering of the march, an attack seemed insane. But Clark had a trick in mind. He sent the Frenchman into town to announce that all French residents who wished to oppose the American army should immediately take cover with Hamilton inside Fort Sackville. The French remained quietly in their homes, watching for the arrival of the Americans.

At sunset on February 23, the residents of Vincennes saw Clark's army approaching the outskirts of town. Clark had his men divided into two companies, which he paraded across the openings between some buildings. When one had passed from view, its men hurried through the woods to form again at the rear of the second. From a distance in the dim light, it appeared that Clark had a long line of companies totaling perhaps a thousand men. Hamilton's Indian allies did a quick calculation of the odds against them and disappeared into the woods.

With drums beating and the French citizens cheering, the Americans marched up the main street to attack Fort Sackville.

Clark ordered siege trenches dug. The British responded with ineffective cannon and musket fire throughout the night. By morning, the Americans had a trench within thirty yards of the fort. Sharp-eyed American marksmen began picking off the British gunners. Clark demanded the fort's surrender. Hamilton refused, then reconsidered and asked for favorable terms. Clark replied that he would accept nothing but complete surrender, adding that he could barely restrain his far superior force from overwhelming the fort and slaughtering all within.

Hamilton considered the warning and gave up. Only when his troops had laid down their arms did he realize what a pitifully small force Clark had brought to Vincennes. In his years of captivity in Virginia, Hamilton must have spent many hours cursing his folly.

Dividing the Wilderness

After Clark's capture of Vincennes, the wilderness war became a bloody standoff. Without enough troops or supplies, Clark never launched an attack on Detroit. Without the ruthlessly capable Hamilton, the British never mounted a campaign to reoccupy the "old Northwest."

At the peace negotiations in Paris, Clark's exploits gave the Americans at least some claim to the wilderness that would one day become the states of Ohio, Indiana, Illinois, Michigan, Wisconsin, and part of Minnesota. The British had at least an equal claim to much of the territory but finally agreed to a northern boundary line running east to west through the Great Lakes.

The draft treaty ending the American Revolution was signed on November 30, 1782. In January 1783, France and Spain made peace with Britain. The final treaty was signed by all parties on September 3, 1783. A new member joined the community of nations, the United States of America.

★ 4 ★

Confederation of Free States

Ideals, blood, and courage had forged a new nation. Yet the thirteen states were far from truly united. Through trial and error, America groped for a form of government that would preserve individual freedoms and, at the same time, ensure safety and prosperity for all citizens.

It was not an easy task. Never before had such a large number of people inhabiting such a vast land announced the intention of governing themselves. History provided numerous political theories but little practical experience in the formation of a great republic.

The State Constitutions

Fortunately, Americans could draw on a long tradition of representative government. Before the Revolution, the citizens of the colonies had elected assemblies to advise the royal governors. During the Revolution, the assemblies had taken control of the colonies, passing laws, raising troops, and electing governors.

All the states adopted constitutions in the war years. The authors examined models suggested by political philosophers down through the ages. None of the plans exactly fit the circumstances in revolutionary America, so the constitution writers made changes. Three different approaches to self-government emerged from the process.

The Virginia Model. Virginia's assembly passed the first state constitution in early 1776. It gave the majority of power to an assembly of two houses (a bicameral legislature). The upper house (the Senate) protected the interests of the wealthy and well educated. The lower house (the House of Delegates) represented the concerns of the common people. The two houses served as a check on each other, preventing either the wealthy or the common people from gaining too much power. Every year, the two houses elected a governor and an eight-member council to carry out the laws passed by the assembly.

The Virginia constitution had faults. The government it established was slow to act and often inefficient. After their bitter experience with royal governors, the constitution writers had given the elected governor little real power. Without the right to veto legislation, the governor became little more than the servant of an assembly that was often too divided to give him clear and timely instructions.

Nor did the constitution give wide representation to the state's people. Following the custom of the day, the Virginia constitution restricted the right to vote to white males who owned at least some property. Most blacks were slaves, the Indians were considered the enemies of white society, and women were expected to serve their husbands and families without concerning themselves with the affairs of the larger world. Within white male society, the ownership of property was the measure of a man. Those who had not succeeded in gaining at least some property were considered too lazy or too stupid to deserve a vote.

Despite its faults, the Virginia constitution worked well enough to become the model for most of the other state constitutions.

Democratic Experiment. Pennsylvania chose a radical form of self-government. Nearly every male in the state was given the right to vote for representatives to the one-chamber (unicameral) assembly. The assembly elected an executive council, whose president served as the chief executive of the state. Although a noble experiment in democracy, Pennsylvania's constitution was a disaster. Without the check of a second house or a governor holding any real power, a lower-class mob grabbed control of the assembly. After that, the assembly spent more effort on looting rich Loyalists and depriving religious minorities of their rights than fairly and efficiently governing the state.

Mixed Government. In the stormy years leading to the Revolution, Massachusetts had known the fear of mob rule, a power grab by the rich, and tyranny by the chief executive. The constitution writers in the Bay State adopted a "mixed" form of government, designed to prevent any class or person from gaining too much power. They gave equal power to a bicameral legislature, a governor elected by the people, and a judicial branch that would interpret laws and resolve disputes between the other two branches. Each branch would "check and balance" the power of the others, providing the state with a just and stable government. The carefully designed constitution should have worked better than it did. Unfortunately, rich merchants seized control of the upper house of the legislature and used its power to block reforms benefiting the majority of the people.

The Continental Congress

Each state sent representatives to the Continental Congress. The Congress had first met in September 1774 to decide on a unified policy for opposing British tyranny. After war broke out in the spring of 1775, Congress found itself forced into the role of a national government. The delegates elected a committee headed by John Dickinson of Delaware to design the framework for a Continental government.

The committee presented Congress with the Articles of Confederation in early July 1776, not long before Congress adopted the Declaration of Independence. The proposed framework for a national government tried to satisfy both large and small states. It did not, and numerous changes were made before the articles were approved by Congress in November 1777. The articles were forwarded to the state assemblies for approval, but the objections of the Maryland assembly to Virginia's claims of vast lands in the West blocked ratification for more than three years.

During this time, America was trying to win a war. Out of necessity, Congress assumed powers that it had no legal right to wield. However, it never dared offend the states by imposing taxes. Instead, Congress made requests for money, men, and supplies. The states often responded with little or nothing.

No one had greater reason for frustration than George Washington. He wrote scores of letters to Congress, begging for better support. His men grew to despise the politicians and talked darkly of marching on Congress to demand their pay. However, Congress could do little without clearly defined powers and the cooperation of the states. On March 1, 1781—little more than seven months before the decisive victory at Yorktown—the Maryland assembly finally passed the Articles of Confederation. At last, the government of the United States had an official basis.

The Articles of Confederation were badly flawed. Still, it was something of a wonder that the thirteen diverse, competing states had agreed to any form of unified government. The articles would serve as the framework of the national government for eight years before the people put them aside in favor of a far wiser constitution.

Fear of Dictatorship

Peace brought new worries. Many people feared that dissatisfied elements in the army would try to take over the government. But George Washington had fought too long and hard to let the "glorious cause" end in a military dictatorship. He faced down the plotters, then respectfully submitted his resignation to Congress: "Having now finished the work assigned me, I retire from the great theatre of action; and bidding an affectionate farewell to [Congress] under whose orders I have so long acted, I here offer my commission, and take my leave of all employments of public life."

Thomas Mifflin, the president of the Congress, expressed the gratitude of the nation: "You have conducted the great military contest with wisdom and fortitude, invariably regarding the rights of the civil power through all disasters and changes."

The choice of words by both speakers emphasized that the military must always obey the elected government ("the civil power"). The United States must be a nation governed by laws, not by guns.

The Confederation

Congress set about governing a nation struggling to recover from years of war. Soon the flaws in the Articles of Confederation became obvious. Each state had one vote in Congress. Tiny Rhode Island and wilderness Georgia had the same power as such large, populous states as Virginia and Pennsylvania. Since nine votes were required to pass a law, the opposition of five small states could block legislation of benefit to the majority of the American people. If a law did pass, a dissenting state could ignore it, since Congress lacked any method of forcing obedience. Even if all states agreed to a law, no federal court system existed to make sure it was uniformly applied in all states.

The articles gave Congress no power to raise funds through taxation. At the minimum, the national government should have had the power to tax and regulate foreign trade. However, the states had reserved that power for themselves. A tangle of state customs regulations soon played havoc with foreign trade. Even worse, states began imposing taxes on trade with neighboring states. Small states were particularly hard hit. Prosperous New Jersey saw its wealth drained by the high taxes New York and Pennsylvania imposed on imports from other states.

The articles established five executive departments: foreign affairs, finance, war, an admiralty (maritime affairs) board, and a post office. Yet there was no chief executive to coordinate the executive functions. When sitting, Congress as a whole served as the chief executive. When Congress was not in session, a committee of one delegate from each state supervised the government.

All the flaws in the articles might have been repaired except for one final, glaring stupidity: the articles could not be amended without the approval of *all* the states. That provision doomed the Articles of Confederation.

Europe Watches

The great powers of Europe waited for the new nation to tear itself apart. France, Spain, and Britain all hoped to add the pieces to their empires.

America's wartime alliances with France and Spain had not led to lasting friendships. Despite the recent hostilities, Britain remained America's natural trading partner and potential ally. In the postwar years, America's ambassador to Britain, John Adams, sought to restore cordial relations. He was frustrated by several complicated disputes.

Under the peace treaty, America had agreed to pay the Loyalists for property taken during the war, but the individual states were slow to make good on the promise. The United States had also agreed not to interfere with the collection of millions of dollars in prewar debts owed by American merchants to British businesses and banks. However, several of the southern states refused to pressure their citizens to pay.

Britain retaliated by refusing to evacuate outposts in the Great Lakes region. As a result, Canadians continued to control the profitable fur trade with the Indians. The standoff grew bitter. American settlers on the frontier accused British agents of stirring up the Indians. The British hotly denied any part in the continuing troubles. As tensions rose, there was danger of a new war between Britain and America.

Spain Grabs for Land

Spanish ambitions in the Mississippi valley and along the Gulf of Mexico presented another problem for the new nation. Spain held title to Florida, New Orleans, and the lands west of the Mississippi. In addition, Spain claimed nearly all the land from the east bank of the river to the Appalachians.

Control of New Orleans gave Spain a powerful means of pressuring the American settlers in the West. The settlers found it far easier to ship their goods down the Mississippi than across the nearly roadless wilderness that separated the frontier from the settled East. Every time Spain threatened to cut off trade through New Orleans, the American settlements along the river and its tributaries faced disaster. The Spanish authorities in New Orleans increased the pressure by encouraging the southern Indian tribes to fight the spread of settlement. Under the threat of Indian attack and economic disaster, many settlers felt abandoned by a do-nothing Congress. Some began talking of breaking away from the United States and seeking protection within the Spanish Empire.

The States Bicker

While the British and Spanish intrigued, the states bickered among themselves. Every state with a western boundary claimed territory in the vast wilderness. The few states without frontier borders had companies buying land from the Indians. Rival land claims were only part of the problem. Northern states feared that the already large southern states would expand until they dominated the Confederation. Eastern merchants, fearing the competition of a settled West, wanted to slow development. In short, the entire western lands dispute was a fantastic mess.

By the mid-1780s, Congress seemed powerless to resolve even the smallest disputes between the states. For years, free use of the Potomac river had been a sore point between Maryland and Virginia. In 1784, the two states almost came to blows in the so-called "oyster war." Maryland oystermen wanted to work the Virginia side of the Potomac River, but Virginia's oystermen threatened to repel any "foreign" invasion with force.

The enemies of America's glorious experiment in self-government must have laughed on hearing of the oyster war. However, a youthful member of Virginia's House of Delegates would turn the farcical dispute into a grand opportunity.

James Madison

At thirty-three, James Madison was a small, slender bachelor—"no bigger than half a piece of soap." Yet no wise man dismissed him lightly. Madison had courage, energy, and perhaps the finest political mind in America. He was embarrassed and maddened by the powerlessness of Congress. Somehow the states must find a way to strengthen the national government, or else watch the Confederation come apart over something as silly as the oyster war.

At Madison's suggestion, the Virginia assembly invited Maryland to send a delegation to a conference at Mount Vernon, Washington's plantation. Maryland accepted. In the dignified atmosphere that always seemed to surround the general, the delegations worked out an agreement on the Potomac disputes. The success of the Mount Vernon conference inspired Madison to suggest a convention of all the states to discuss the commercial problems plaguing the Confederation.

Nine states agreed to send delegations to a convention at Annapolis, Maryland. However, only the delegates from New York, New Jersey, Pennsylvania, Delaware, and Virginia arrived for the opening of the conference in September 1786. A convention of only five states could decide little of importance, but it gave the delegates an opportunity to discuss the poor health of the nation. At Madison's urging, they sent a resolution to Congress, calling for a convention of all the states to revise the Articles of Confederation.

Shays's Rebellion

The resolution from Annapolis reached Congress about the same time as news of a rebellion by poor farmers in western Massachusetts. In other states, governments had helped farmers over the hard times following the Revolution by lending them paper money for the payment of debts. In Massachusetts, however, the powerful eastern merchants insisted that all debts must be paid in scarce gold or silver. By the fall of 1786, many farmers were on the brink of losing their property for nonpayment of private debts and the state's heavy taxes. They rebelled, pushing forward as their none-too-willing leader one Daniel Shays, a former army officer.

The state militia put down the uprising with ease and little loss of life. Shays escaped to Vermont, and the rebellion's other leaders were pardoned or given short jail terms. Still, Shays's Rebellion demonstrated how fragile law and order were in America. New voices were soon calling for a stronger Confederation.

On February 21, 1787, Congress gave its approval to the Annapolis Convention's resolution by urging all states to send representatives to a convention in Philadelphia the following May. At his home in Montpelier, Virginia, "Little Jemmy" Madison began preparing for a summer that would make him one of the towering figures in American history.

Daniel Shays, a former army officer, leads impoverished farmers in their refusal to pay their debts and taxes.

★ 5 ★

The Constitutional Convention

Summer heat already lay on Philadelphia when the delegates to the Constitutional Convention began arriving in the first weeks of May 1787. Longtime residents of America's largest city said it was the warmest spring since 1750. To add to the discomfort, flies had arrived in record numbers to feast on the manure and refuse lying in the streets of this bustling metropolis of forty-three thousand people.

Twelve states had agreed to send delegates to discuss revising the Articles of Confederation. Fiercely independent Rhode Island had refused. Its state government was controlled by a debtor party that was forcing creditors to accept nearly worthless paper currency in payment for debts. The debtor party wanted no part in a federal government that might put strict controls on commercial dealings.

Since each state would have only a single vote in the Convention, Congress had placed no limit on the size of delegations. Pennsylvania sent eight delegates, Virginia seven, and Connecticut and New York three each. The honor of having the smallest delegation would go to New Hampshire when its two representatives finally arrived late in July.

The Delegates

In all, fifty-five men would take part in the Convention. George Washington and Benjamin Franklin were by far the most famous, but most of the others were well known for their service to the young nation. Twenty-one had served in the army during the Revolution. Seven had been state governors. Forty-two had served in Congress and most of the others in state assemblies. Many had taken a hand in writing their state constitutions.

Almost all the delegates had solid educations and several were notable scholars. Thirty-four had legal training and twenty-one practiced law. Among the others, eighteen were planters or farmers, seven were merchants, and nine had other connections with the active commercial and political life of the nation.

Despite their wealth of experience, the delegates were a surprisingly young group. Four were under thirty, only four over sixty. Most were in their mid-thirties to early forties. Only Franklin, at eighty-one, could be called ancient—a fact he pointed out with glee.

With few exceptions, the delegates were open-minded and dedicated men. They had strong opinions, but they were willing to listen to the arguments of others and perhaps change their minds for the good of America. Nearly all agreed that the government must be strengthened in the face of threats from abroad and problems at home. Yet, what form that government should take was far less clear. It would take months of debate to find an answer.

Hopes and Fears

The nation would wait anxiously for the outcome. Most of the people had high hopes, but others feared that the Convention would devise a government so strong that it might destroy the freedoms won in the Revolution. Patrick Henry, Virginia's famous orator, had refused a place in the Virginia delegation, saying he "smelt a rat." Samuel Adams and John Hancock, the fiery Boston revolutionaries, were likewise suspicious and stayed home.

Other famous patriots wanted to attend the Convention but could not. John Jay had his hands full as the secretary for foreign affairs. John Adams was representing the United States in Britain. Thomas Jefferson was ambassador to France. All three were deeply interested in constitutional questions and sent scores of books and countless letters to their friends among the delegates.

George Washington had not wanted to come to Philadelphia. Since the war he had been happy to stay close to his beloved Mount Vernon and his devoted wife, Martha. But James Madison and other friends had insisted that Washington's duty lay in Philadelphia. Reluctantly, he had agreed. In the city, he accepted lodgings in the home of his old friend, Robert Morris, a wealthy delegate from Pennsylvania. But Washington's heart remained elsewhere, and he filled his letters home with instructions on the running of the plantation.

Delayed Opening

The Convention was scheduled to open May 14, but not enough states were represented when the day arrived. James Madison used the delay to good advantage. Every morning, he and the other Virginia delegates worked on proposals to submit to the Convention. In the afternoons, they met with the Pennsylvania delegation to exchange ideas. In the evenings, small groups of delegates met in homes and inns for yet more talk. Madison seemed always among them, prodding and convincing. By the time the Convention opened, Madison had a firm plan and allies to support it.

Nine state delegations had arrived by May 25. The Convention opened in the Pennsylvania State House, a handsome building with large chambers and high ceilings. The delegates took places at tables covered with green cloth, facing a raised platform where a presiding officer would sit. There was no doubt who that officer would be; the delegates elected Washington by a unanimous vote. Madison recorded the fact in the detailed journal he would keep for the next four months.

Washington rose and delivered a short, modest thanks. It would be his last speech until the final day of the Convention. Throughout the long months to come, he would listen carefully, speaking only when he had to rule on matters of procedure. Yet his influence would be great. Delegates would watch his face for a hint of approval or disapproval. His quiet dignity would keep the debate within bounds even when tempers rose.

The Convention approved a set of simple rules. The most important was the rule requiring the delegates to keep silent about the Convention's proceedings. The Convention must have the privacy to hammer out compromises before answering to the newspapers and the public.

The Virginia Plan

After a weekend recess, the Convention reconvened. Edmund Randolph, the handsome, thirty-three-year-old governor of Virginia, rose to present the plan Madison had worked out. Everyone in the room soon realized that Virginia was suggesting not simply a revision of the Articles of Confederation but an entirely new constitution. In fourteen resolutions, the Virginia Plan laid out a framework for a strong central government. A bicameral national legislature (Congress) would have sweeping powers. Its lower house (the House of Representatives) would be elected by the people. The lower house would in turn elect the upper house (the Senate) from nominations made by the state assemblies. Together, the two houses would elect a chief executive, federal judges, and a "council of revision" with the power to revise or reject laws passed by the Congress.

The Virginia Plan horrified most of the delegates from the small states. The Articles of Confederation had given all states equal standing in the Continental Congress. But the Virginia Plan stated that the number of seats in both houses of the new Congress would be awarded according to population. With a clear majority of seats in Congress, the large states would control the government. The executive and judicial branches would do their bidding. The small states would lose influence—perhaps even their independence.

Large and small states lined up for and against the Virginia Plan. With nearly half the American population, Virginia, Pennsylvania, and Massachusetts had the most to gain from the plan. Georgia and the two Carolinas, with hopes of rapid growth, generally favored the plan, but strayed to the other side on some points.

Delaware, New Jersey, Connecticut, and Maryland opposed the plan. New York—a large state in size and population but not in outlook—usually sided with them. The New York delegation was at odds from the beginning, two of its members favoring the small-state position and one—the brilliant Alexander Hamilton—passionately in favor of the large-state position.

With the Convention almost evenly divided, one or two states could throw a vote either way. But Madison's strategy had established the outlines of the debate in favor of the large states. For the next two weeks, the small states would have to argue against the Virginia Plan, instead of proposing their own.

Committee of the Whole

The debate was conducted with all the delegates meeting as a "committee of the whole," rather than in formal session. This procedure took pressure off the delegates. Frequent test votes could be taken to determine the changing mood of the Convention. As the debate brought up new arguments, delegates could reconsider and switch positions without embarrassment, since their earlier votes were not part of the public record. And, if the Convention got stuck on a troublesome point, it could move on to another issue.

The "committee of the whole" procedure required patience. When the time came to formalize a vote in regular session, new questions were usually raised. Often, the delegates found themselves starting a lengthy debate all over again. At times during the summer, it would seem that the delegates were doomed to argue some issues well into the next century.

The small states did not disagree with everything in the Virginia Plan. The Convention quickly approved a government of three branches: legislative, executive, and judicial. The awkward "council of revision" was rejected. A resolution requiring that all states have a republican form of government passed unanimously.

For a time, the delegates debated whether the government should have a single chief executive or several. Many of the delegates worried about giving one man too much power; America did not want another king. They also worried that a single executive would favor his home state and region. Both dangers could be avoided by electing a board of three or more executives representing different regions of the country. Still, could a committee carry out the executive functions efficiently? The delegates decided it could not. Over the objections of New York, Maryland, Delaware, and several prominent delegates from other states, the Convention decided that the nation should have a single chief executive.

With surprising ease, the committee of the whole approved awarding seats in the House of Representatives according to population. However, the small states blocked a similar arrangement for the Senate. Connecticut proposed giving each state equal representation in the Senate. The large states rejected the idea. It was an issue that would become the most troublesome of the summer, coming up again and again until it threatened to destroy the Convention.

The Convention let the matter drop for the time being and moved on to consider whether the Senate should be appointed by the president or elected by the Congress, the state legislatures, or the people. Franklin and others argued that the people should be trusted with the responsibility, but the Convention decided to give the power to the state legislatures.

By the middle of June, the Convention had worked its way through the Virginia Plan, accepting some parts, rejecting others, and delaying debate on the rest. Much remained to do, but the Constitution had begun to take shape. And the small states did not like what they saw.

The New Jersey Plan

On June 15, William Paterson of New Jersey rose to present the small states' alternative to the Virginia Plan. The New Jersey Plan called for a unicameral Congress with each state equally represented. The state legislatures, not the people, would select the representatives. An executive branch headed by not one but three officers would carry out the laws passed by Congress. The judicial branch would be small and weak.

The New Jersey Plan was little more than an updated version of the Articles of Confederation with many of the weaknesses intact. Yet, as Paterson pointed out, the Convention had been called to *revise* the articles, not to replace them. The changes proposed by the New Jersey Plan would increase the efficiency of the national government but leave the majority of the power in the hands of the independent and *equal* states.

James Wilson of Pennsylvania responded for the large states. Wilson has been called "the unsung hero of the Convention." Like eleven other delegates, he was foreign-born and still spoke with the Scottish brogue of his homeland. Wilson had served in Congress, signed the Declaration of Independence, and earned a reputation as a brilliant legal scholar. In the Convention, he had become Madison's closest ally.

An outsider might not have been impressed to see Wilson take the floor. At forty-five, Wilson had narrow shoulders, a pudgy face, and glasses perched low on his nose. But Wilson's looks disguised the man inside. A colleague described Wilson's mind as "one blaze of light."

Wilson tore into the New Jersey Plan with all the awesome power of his intelligence. He did not shout, threaten, or hurl fiery phrases at the Convention. His words were cold, reasoned, ruthless. He dismissed Paterson's argument that the Convention could only "revise" the Articles of Confederation by stating that the delegates could "conclude nothing" but were "at liberty to propose *anything.*" With that small-state argument neatly punctured, he delivered a devastating point-by-point comparison of the two plans.

On June 19, Madison took his turn. His cool, logical speech left the small-state plan in tatters. The clerk called the vote and recorded only New Jersey and New York in favor of the New Jersey Plan. It had been a critical few days. In some ways the New Jersey Plan had represented an easy way out for the delegates. By rejecting it, the Convention had declared its intention to carry through with the difficult task of writing a completely new constitution.

The Great Debate

Weeks of hard work and hard bargaining lay ahead. On June 20, the Convention went into formal session to reconsider the decisions it had made as a committee of the whole.

After a week of debating other matters, the Convention turned again to the difficult question of how to award seats in the Senate. The large states argued that they should have more seats because of their greater populations. How else could the majority of the American people be fairly represented? The small states argued that all states should have an equal vote. How else could the small states protect their citizens from the greed and power of the large states?

For two weeks the debate raged as the delegates sweated in the stuffy chamber and the flies buzzed beyond the closed shutters. Luther Martin of Maryland—"the wild man of the Convention"—delivered long, tangled speeches against a too-powerful national government. Wilson, Madison, and Gouverneur Morris of Pennsylvania delivered cutting replies. The debate turned ugly. Gunning Bedford of Delaware let fly a snarling attack on the large states: "They insist . . . they never will hurt or injure the lesser states. *I do not, gentlemen, trust you!*"

Further angry words could destroy the Convention. Other delegates rose to urge calm. Elbridge Gerry of Massachusetts cautioned: "If we do not come to some agreement among ourselves, some foreign sword will probably do the work for us."

The Good Doctor

Through all the long days of debate, Benjamin Franklin had a steadying influence on the Convention. Probably no one suffered more from the heat and the strain of sitting through the endless speeches. At eighty-one, the "good doctor" was in such poor health that he had to be carried to the State House every morning in a sedan chair by four strapping prisoners of the town jail. He no longer had the strength to stand for more than a few minutes, and James Wilson volunteered to read most of Franklin's speeches. Yet, day after day, Franklin took his seat in the chamber. His good humor and calm wisdom never seemed to fail. Many delegates who might have taken an excuse to slip or stomp out of the Convention stayed because of Franklin's example.

By July 2, further debate seemed pointless. The Connecticut proposal to give each state an equal vote in the Senate was brought to a vote. The Convention's reporter recorded the tally: five states for; five states against; Georgia split. Stalemate. Gloom fell on the Convention. Without a compromise on this critical issue, the Constitution could not be written. Exhausted, the delegates selected a "grand committee" to study the matter, then adjourned for the Fourth of July.

The Crisis

Philadelphia celebrated the Declaration of Independence with parades, cannon salutes, and speeches in praise of freedom and democracy. People drank countless toasts to the delegates and the great Constitution such worthy men were sure to produce.

Few of the delegates had much enthusiasm for the festivities. They had come to Philadelphia six weeks before determined to give America a government worthy of its future. Almost to a man, they believed that America's great experiment in self-government represented a bright hope in a world governed mostly by kings. George Mason of Virginia spoke for many when he announced that he would rather see his bones buried in Philadelphia than go home without a constitution. But now all their hopes, determination, and hard work seemed about to go for nothing.

On July 5, the delegates assembled to hear the grand committee's report. No one was happy with it. Glumly, the delegates once more set to work. They formed new committees, argued once-decided issues all over again, and tried to find some way to resolve the biggest issue of all—representation in the Senate. According to one observer, Washington's face had the same grim expression he had worn in the bleak winter at Valley Forge, when the Revolution seemed all but lost.

On July 10, the two remaining delegates from New York walked out in disgust, leaving only ten states represented in the Convention. Washington wrote to Alexander Hamilton, who had left ten days earlier on private business: "I wish you were back.

. . . I almost despair of seeing a favorable [conclusion] to the proceedings."

"The Great Compromise"

Men of less dedication might have given up, but the delegates pressed on. No one realized it at first, but each small compromise served to tie more delegates to the larger framework of the Constitution. Some of the large-state delegates, including Franklin and Mason, began to lean toward giving the small states equal representation in the Senate, rather than pass no constitution at all.

On July 16—a cool day for a change—the Convention finished revising the grand committee's report. Its critical provision awarded seats in the lower house of Congress according to a state's population but gave all states equal representation in the Senate. The reporter called the vote: Delaware, Maryland, Connecticut, New Jersey, and North Carolina in favor; Pennsylvania, Virginia, South Carolina, and Georgia opposed; Massachusetts divided; New York absent. The measure carried 5–4.

Historians would call it "the Great Compromise." In many ways, it was less a compromise than a defeat for the large states. Yet, it was also a victory for everyone, since it guaranteed that the Constitution *would* be written. The large states considered renewing the fight but then let the matter drop. The Convention moved on to other issues.

After the Great Compromise, the small-state/large-state alliances broke apart, and the delegates became more ready to compromise. They debated what powers the Congress should have, different methods for ratifying the Constitution, and the hottest remaining issue—how the president should be elected and what powers he should wield. New Hampshire's delegates finally arrived. Alexander Hamilton returned to give New York at least some say in the debate.

Power and the People

The question of how to elect a president was tied up with the whole issue of how much power to grant to the people. Many delegates distrusted people of little education or property. Elbridge Gerry of Massachusetts shrilly reminded the delegates of Shays's Rebellion and the dangers of mob rule. The brilliant Gouverneur Morris of Pennsylvania and the wise John Dickinson of Delaware were among those who also favored restricting the vote to "men of property and responsibility."

On the other side, Franklin, Wilson, Mason, and—after a little hesitation—Madison spoke for giving the people the maximum say in their government. Power and responsibility would make the people wise. It was far better, they argued, to trust the people to elect the best man president than to leave it to state or national legislators, who might take bribes or make shady deals.

The delegates wrestled with the problem of how to elect the president throughout the summer. Everyone knew that the man destined to be the first president sat quietly among them. But what would happen after Washington stepped down? Would a few large states push their candidate on the rest of the nation? Or would small states gang up on the large? Would it become a fight between North and South? Or someday between East and West? Some fifty times, the delegates voted on different methods of electing the president. Not until the final days of the Convention would they reach a compromise.

Committee of Detail

By the third week in July, the Convention had decided dozens of questions and needed to examine how all the decisions fit together. On July 26, the Convention appointed a "committee of detail" to compose a rough draft of the Constitution.

While the committee labored, the rest of the delegates took a needed break. Some returned to their homes, others found amusement in the surrounding countryside. Washington went trout fishing near Valley Forge, where his army had spent the terrible winter of 1777–1778. He wrote in his diary that the buckwheat growing on the site would make excellent feed for the hogs and horses at Mount Vernon.

In Philadelphia, the committee of detail hammered out the rough draft. The committee's five members—Edmund Randolph of Virginia, James Wilson of Pennsylvania, Nathaniel Gorham of Massachusetts, Oliver Ellsworth of Connecticut, and John Rutledge of South Carolina—worked well together. They sketched the framework of the new government in spare, careful language, leaving out unnecessary details that might create confusion.

The weeks of debate had greatly altered the original Virginia Plan. The Congress would no longer hold most of the power. Instead, the three branches of government would be equal, each serving as a "check and balance" on the other two. It would not be the most efficient form of government, but it would be durable.

On August 6, the Convention reconvened. The committee of detail presented its rough draft. For the next three weeks, the delegates worked their way through the draft—adding, revising, and rejecting provisions.

Slavery

A difficult issue remained for the delegates to consider—slavery. In the North, where slavery had never had deep roots, several states had banned or were on the point of outlawing slavery. Yet northern merchants and shipowners were still making fortunes in the slave trade. In the South, slavery was considered necessary to the well-being of the region's economy. Yet, even some of the Convention's nineteen slave-owning delegates were uncomfortable with the institution. George Mason of Virginia, a slave-owner and Washington's close friend, warned the Convention that slavery would bring "the judgment of heaven" on America.

No amount of debate could alter the brutal fact that any attempt to abolish slavery or the slave trade was likely to wreck the Constitution. Georgia, South Carolina, and probably other southern states would refuse to ratify it. Furthermore, the southern states demanded that their slave populations count in some way in determining how many seats they would receive in the House of Representatives.

In all likelihood, a solid majority of the delegates detested slavery. Yet they had to make a compromise or see the Constitution come unstuck. They gritted their teeth and made a deal. Each state would be left to decide if slavery would be allowed within its borders. The slave trade would be allowed to continue until 1808, when Congress could decide to ban it. A slave would count as three-fifths of a white person in determining representation in the House and for the calculation of taxes.

It was no doubt the Convention's low point. The delegates had chosen politics over morality. Yet, most of them would agree with Madison when he wrote: "Great as the evil is, a dismemberment of the Union would be worse."

Impatient for the End

The delegates were tired and ready to go home, but other matters remained unsettled. Defining eligibility for office took some time. The Convention set minimum age requirements and voted to open all offices except the presidency to men of foreign birth after they had resided in the United States for a suitable time. It voted down a final attempt to restrict officeholding to men of considerable property, but left it to the states to establish qualifications for voters.

The subject of a religious test for officeholding came up again but was quickly dismissed. The delegates held a range of religious views, and the majority wanted no part in establishing a state church or state attitude toward religion. Let basic human morality protect the republic.

The issue of selecting a capital city took further time. When it became obvious that every region wanted the honor and the benefits, the delegates decided to leave the matter to Congress.

Finally, the delegates turned again to the ratification issue. How many states would need to ratify the Constitution before it became the law of the United States? A unanimous vote seemed unlikely, and James Wilson convinced the Convention to set the figure at nine. Should a state's legislature or its people decide to accept or reject the Constitution? Madison, Wilson, and George Mason argued strongly for giving the responsibility to the people. Let the people speak by electing delegates to special ratification conventions. Their plan was approved.

Unfinished Business

On the last day of August, the Convention turned a few remaining matters over to yet one more committee. The "committee on unfinished parts" defined the taxing power of the Congress, reduced the duties of the Senate, and worked out a final compromise on the problem of electing a president.

The president would be elected by an electoral college made up of delegates selected by the state legislatures. Each state would have an electoral vote equal to its total number of seats in the House and Senate. If no candidate received a majority of the electoral vote, the House of Representatives would choose a president and the Senate a vice president from among the leading candidates. It was a poor solution, probably the most awkward in the Constitution, but it satisfied the delegates.

Style and Arrangement

A "committee on style and arrangement" took over on September 8. Its members were William Johnson of Connecticut, Alexander Hamilton of New York, James Madison of Virginia, Rufus King of Massachusetts, and Gouverneur Morris of Pennsylvania. Morris was a particularly skilled writer, and the final draft was largely his work. He cut away the excess words, reorganized the provisions, and rewrote the introduction.

On September 12, a sweltering Wednesday, the committee presented its work to the Convention. The delegates took a deep breath of the chamber's stale air and set about reviewing the Constitution word by word. For four more days they worked. A few changes were approved, most voted down. Friday it rained. Some of the delegates began to have doubts about the wisdom of the Constitution. Among them were Edmund Randolph, who had proposed the original Virginia Plan, and George Mason, who had sworn to leave his bones in Philadelphia rather than quit.

Determined to put an end to the work, the Convention stayed

in session late on Saturday. Randolph and Mason proposed holding a second convention to answer any objections the states might have. Other delegates spoke strongly against the idea. A second convention could undo all the careful work of the first. The Constitution already contained a reasonable procedure for voting amendments. Let the states accept or reject the Constitution as written and change what needed changing later on. Randolph and Mason's motion lost 12–0.

The time had come at last to vote on the Constitution. The reporter called the role of the states. James Madison wrote in his journal: "All states aye."

The Signing

A clear, cold morning brought a hint of autumn to Philadelphia on Monday, September 17, 1787. The forty remaining delegates took their places in the chamber for the final day of the Convention. James Wilson read a speech by Dr. Franklin: "Mr. President, I confess that there are several parts of this Constitution which I do not at present approve. . . . But I am not sure I shall never approve them. . . . The older I grow, the more apt I am to doubt my own judgment, and to pay more respect to the judgment of others. . . . I consent, Sir, to this Constitution, because I expect no better and because I am not sure that it is not the best." The speech concluded by urging all members to put their objections aside and sign.

Nathaniel Gorham of Massachusetts requested a change that would give a seat in the House of Representatives to every thirty thousand people, rather than every forty thousand. Probably to hurry things along, Washington seconded Gorham's motion with a brief speech—his first in all the long months. The Convention approved the change. A few other members spoke. Randolph

The signing of the Constitution in 1787

and Mason said they were sorry, but they would not sign without a provision for a second convention. They were joined by only one other delegate, Elbridge Gerry of Massachusetts, who—as usual—had a long list of complaints.

Finally, at three in the afternoon, the signing began with the delegates moving to the front table according to the order of the states from north to south. When Pennsylvania's turn came, Franklin was helped to the front. Observers said the old man wept as he signed.

Back in his seat, Franklin spoke quietly to Madison and a few other delegates nearby. He referred to the sun painted on the back of the president's chair: "I have often and often . . . looked at [it] . . . without being able to tell whether it was rising or setting. But now at length I have the happiness to know that it is a rising and not a setting sun."

Franklin was right—a new day was dawning for America.

★ 6 ★

―――――"We the People..."―――――

The Constitution began: "We the People of the United States of America . . ." These simple words spoke volumes. The Constitution and the government it proposed were to belong to the people. It would be their choice to accept or reject the Convention's work. And if they ratified it, they could expect both the benefits and the responsibilities of self-government.

To the States

Three days after the signing, the Constitution reached New York City, where the Continental Congress was in session. The Congress spent only a few days reviewing the Constitution before forwarding it to the states.

Meanwhile, the Constitution was published throughout the country. It startled most Americans. They had expected a constitution that would strengthen the Confederation, not establish a completely new government. Some people reacted with delight, others with fear. Politicians hurried to embrace or attack the Constitution in newspapers and speeches.

Federalists and Antifederalists

The debate over the Constitution split the people into two groups. The Federalists favored the Constitution and the strong Union, or federation, it proposed. The Antifederalists declared that they were also in favor of Union, but not in the form the Constitution outlined. The Antifederalists were not stupid or unpatriotic. They genuinely believed that the Constitution endangered the hard-won freedoms of the Revolution.

In the ratification debate, the Antifederalists were at a disadvantage. They had no unified organization or common plan to offer in place of the Constitution. Their only hope lay in appealing to the people's fears: The new government would be too strong. Not enough power had been left to the states. The government would impose heavy trade duties and enforce their collection with an army. Without a list of guaranteed individual freedoms—a bill of rights—in the Constitution, the federal government could become a tyrant worse than the king and Parliament of Britain.

The Federalists were ready for the attacks. Their main spokesmen had served in the Convention and had listened to all these arguments before. They cited the checks and balances in the Constitution; explained how the states would be equal partners in the new system; and justified the government's taxing and regulation powers by pointing to the bankruptcy of the Confederation and the chaos of state trade regulations. Only when they had to address the lack of a bill of rights did their arguments falter.

As the time for elections approached, the debate got nasty. Patrick Henry's thundering attacks on the Constitution rocked Virginia. In Maryland, Luther Martin, who had stomped out of the Convention, delivered snarling assaults. Elbridge Gerry of Massachusetts, who had stayed until the last day before refusing to sign, tore into the Constitution with his long list of objections. The Federalists answered with their own strong words. A number of delegates who had signed the Constitution with mixed feelings found themselves warming to its defense.

Despite the hot language, the debate produced little real violence. No one was tossed in jail for speaking out. There were demonstrations but no riots. The army kept to its quarters; the veterans left their muskets hung on the wall. Other nations were impressed by the orderliness of the debate in a country so used to revolution.

The Federalist Papers

Beginning in late October 1787, newspaper readers began seeing articles signed "Publius." In clear, eloquent language, the articles explained nearly every aspect of the Constitution. What would become known as the Federalist Papers were written not by the fictional Publius, but by the brilliant team of Alexander Hamilton, John Jay, and James Madison.

Federalist Paper 10, written by Madison, assured the people that they need not fear a large, strong republic. Many points of view would be represented in the government. The range of competing interests, or factions, would be the strength of the republic. It would be nearly impossible for one faction to impose its will on all the others. It would be almost equally difficult for a number of competing factions to form a majority so strong that it could deprive a minority of its rights.

Thousands of ordinary people read and discussed the Federalist Papers and became convinced of the wisdom of the Constitution. Their fears quieted, they began to appreciate the vision of a strong, united nation expanding westward. The United States did not have to be a weak collection of bickering states. Under its new Constitution, it could become the equal of any nation on earth.

The Conventions Open

The tide was running in favor of the Federalists by the time the state conventions began meeting in late autumn 1787. Yet each state had its own concerns, and the Antifederalists were far from beaten. Their best argument against the Constitution was its lack of a bill of rights. The people should have guarantees of freedom of religion, freedom of speech, the right to a fair trial, the right to hold political meetings, and so on. Most of the state constitutions included such bills of rights, why didn't the Constitution? Was a plot afoot to rob the people of their freedoms?

In truth, the Convention had blundered. A bill of rights had been discussed, but in their fatigue the delegates had failed to see the need to include rights already guaranteed by the states. Although the Federalists now saw the error, they worried that the state conventions might start changing the Constitution, then voting not on the original but on the amended document. The result could be a dozen different versions for a second Constitutional Convention to reconcile. Another Convention and another round of ratification proceedings could take years. The Federalists argued that America could not waste the time. Let the states pass the Constitution as written, and the Federalists would back amendments adding a bill of rights.

The States Vote

On December 7, 1787, Delaware's convention became the first to put the Constitution to a vote. Debate in the second smallest state had been quiet. The Constitution would protect Delaware from its powerful neighbors and promote the state's thriving trade. The delegates voted unanimously in favor of ratification.

Debate in Pennsylvania was far more lively. Pennsylvania had the most radical of the state constitutions and a long history of stormy politics. Its convention sat for five weeks. James Wilson led the Federalist side. Day in and day out, he explained the reasoning behind the Constitution and argued its merits. On December 12, the convention approved the Constitution by a two-to-one margin.

In the next month, three more states voted for ratification. New Jersey and Connecticut saw themselves in much the same position as Delaware. New Jersey approved unanimously, Connecticut by a comfortable three-to-one margin. Georgia, lightly settled and isolated at the southern end of the country, needed federal protection. It passed the Constitution with a unanimous vote.

The Constitution had five of the nine votes it needed for ratification. Massachusetts added the sixth. The Antifederalists recruited many of the state's westerners, who had sympathized with Shays's Rebellion and distrusted government in general. The Federalists sought the support of the eastern merchants and tradesmen, who would prosper under a strong, stable government. With difficulty, the Federalists also won the backing of Samuel Adams and Governor John Hancock, who had both been suspicious of the Constitutional Convention. The popular Hancock agreed to push for ratification if the state convention could forward a list of *nonbinding* changes for Congress to accept or reject. The strategy convinced just enough undecided delegates. Early in February 1788, the Massachusetts convention approved the Constitution 187–168, and the constitution edged a step closer to ratification.

Two states seemed unlikely to ratify. Rhode Island continued to go its own stubborn way. In North Carolina, fears of a strong federal government and the lack of a bill of rights delayed a final decision for many months. Other states followed Massachusetts's example of voting approval with nonbinding suggestions. In April, Maryland joined its small-state cousins, ratifying the Constitution by a wide margin. South Carolina voted in May. The state had heavy war debts that the federal government would assume and, like Georgia, felt the need for military protection. The Constitution passed in South Carolina by more than two to one.

It fell to the rugged individualists of New Hampshire to give the Constitution the vote it needed to become the law of the land. Despite a deep-seated distrust of strong government and a hatred of slavery, the delegates voted approval on June 21, 1788, by a narrow 57–47 vote.

Virginia and New York

The Constitution had won the approval of the necessary nine states. However, everyone knew that Virginia and New York must vote in favor to make a national government workable.

The debate in Virginia had been raging for months. Nowhere were the Antifederalists better organized or led by men of greater fame and ability. Patrick Henry thundered. George Mason, who had regretfully refused to sign the Constitution, listed convincing objections. A score of other prominent Virginians, including James Monroe, a future president, sided with them.

The Federalists had men of equal ability. James Madison worked himself to exhaustion defending his beloved Constitution. Edmund Randolph examined his soul and declared that he had been mistaken in refusing to sign. Converted, Randolph was brilliant in debate. John Marshall, who would become a powerful chief justice of the United States Supreme Court, added the weight of his intelligence and charm to the fight.

George Washington distanced himself from the Virginia convention. He was sensitive to the fact that he would almost certainly be the nation's first president. He needed to stay above the spats on the convention floor if he were to unify the country later on. But Washington was not idle at Mount Vernon. He met with visiting Federalists and Antifederalists, wrote a flood of letters on behalf of the Constitution, and kept careful track of the ratification process throughout the country.

On June 25, the Constitution came to a vote in the Virginia convention. It passed 89–79. That evening, a crowd of angry Antifederalists gathered to plan a revolt. Instead of issuing a fiery call to action, Patrick Henry spoke quietly: He had fought as hard as he could, but a majority of the people's representatives had voted to ratify the Constitution. It was time for the Antifederalists to return to their homes and prepare to support the new government. No other course lay open to true believers in democracy. The crowd broke up quietly.

News of Virginia's vote reached New York's convention a week later. The debate had been hot in New York, with the Antifederalists holding the upper hand from the first. Alexander Hamilton had led the uneven fight for the Constitution. His arguments were brilliant, his energy almost superhuman. The convention wavered. The news from Virginia tipped the balance. On July 26, New York approved the Constitution by a three-vote margin, 30–27. Government under the Constitution could begin.

The New Government

George Washington was chosen by a unanimous vote to become the first president under the Constitution. He took office April 30, 1789. Seven months later, North Carolina ratified the Constitution. Rhode Island held out until the following spring, joining the Union only after the national government threatened to break trade ties with the smallest state.

In all the states, the vast majority of Antifederalists took their defeat with grace. They turned their talents to making the new government a success. Patrick Henry helped promote the Bill of Rights. James Madison, his enemy in the ratification debate, pushed the Bill of Rights through Congress. In 1791, the Bill of Rights became the first ten amendments to the Constitution.

Europe Takes Notice

The great nations of Europe took notice of the new confidence the Constitution gave America. Instead of breaking apart, the United States seemed destined to grow in strength and unity. Britain and America reopened negotiations on the problems remaining from the Revolution. America agreed to pay the losses suffered by Loyalists and British merchants in the war. The British began a slow evacuation of their outposts on American territory.

Spain continued to intrigue on the southern and western borders until it lost most of its American territories to the French

dictator Napoleon. He would sell the lands west of the Mississippi to the United States in 1803.

The federal government took control of the lands once so hotly contested by the eastern states. As the lands between the Appalachians and the Mississippi filled up, new states were admitted to the Union, most of them according to the procedure laid down in the Ordinance of 1787, one of the great documents in American history.

Also called the Northwest Ordinance, it had been written by the Continental Congress in the same summer the Constitutional Convention was meeting in Philadelphia. The Ordinance outlined a procedure for dividing the lands north of the Ohio River into new states. It guaranteed frontier settlers the political and religious rights enjoyed by citizens in the East. As the population of a proposed state grew, its citizens would gain the right to form a legislature and petition for admission to the Union on an equal footing with the older states. By 1850, eighteen new states would join the Union under the federal guidelines originally laid down in the Northwest Ordinance.

"To Ourselves and Our Posterity . . ."

The Constitution promised republican self-government for the generation of the Revolution and all who followed after. It was

At Federal Hall in New York City, George Washington is sworn in as the first president of the United States of America on April 30, 1789.

a promise that could only be kept by the continuing will and participation of the American people.

As the years passed and the nation grew, the Constitution proved a remarkably enduring document. It was not without flaws, and later generations passed amendments to make it more efficient and just. Slavery was abolished in 1865, following the American Civil War. The people received the right to elect senators in 1913. Women won the right to vote in 1919. Other amendments were added to protect the rights of minorities and the public at large. Still others clarified the powers of the branches of government and dealt with circumstances unimagined by the delegates to the Constitutional Convention.

Some outdated provisions remain two centuries after that long, sweltering summer in Philadelphia. The process of writing the Constitution is not finished. Nor is the task of making America's great democratic experiment work every day and for all the people.

Epilogue
Building a Nation

West of Pittsburgh, the river grew wider by the mile. Cleared land fell away behind, replaced by untamed wilderness. It was a country to make a person feel small. In the trackless woods flanking the mighty Ohio lay unknown dangers—hostile Indians, hungry beasts, poisonous snakes, death in a hundred forms. On the flatboats and rafts, the pioneer families rode amid their possessions—a few tools, some dried food, usually a dog or two, sometimes a goat or a cow. The blades of the long oars dipped into the river, each sweep leaving the settled East and civilization farther astern.

More than a few of the pioneers felt a twinge of regret, a moment of homesickness in these first hours on the river. They would feel it again. Ahead lay rapids, storms, hunger, and countless hours of back-breaking labor. Yet the wilderness offered something worth all the dangers and miseries: opportunity—the opportunity to live by the skill of one's hands, the endurance of the body, and the faith of the spirit.

They had set out to build a new life in the wilderness. They would rarely think of it as nation-building, but that was the inevitable result. Over the generations, the grit and skill of the pioneers would conquer a continent. It would not be a smooth or gentle conquest. The pioneers would trample the rights of the Indians and each other; cut down great forests without a thought for the future; slaughter buffalo until almost none remained. Yet, for all their mistakes, later generations would remember them as heroes—common people who had dared a wilderness and built a nation.

Like the pioneers, the United States would survive its errors and misfortunes. America's great experiment in democracy would inspire millions to cross the oceans to the New World. Peoples of dozens of nations would throw off tyranny to form democracies of their own. They would rewrite in their own languages and to their own tastes those three simple words: "We the People . . ."

Suggested Reading

Bowen, Catherine Drinker. *Miracle at Philadelphia*. Boston: Atlantic Monthly Press, 1966.

Derleth, August. *Vincennes: Portal to the West*. Englewood, New Jersey: Prentice-Hall, 1968.

Ketchum, Richard, ed. *The Revolution*. New York: American Heritage, 1958.

McDowell, Bart. *The Revolutionary War*. Washington: National Geographic Society, 1967.

Middlekauff, Robert. *The Glorious Cause*. New York: Oxford University Press, 1982.

Sgroi, Peter. *. . . this Constitution*. New York: Franklin Watts, 1986.

Ward, Christopher. *The War of the Revolution*. New York: Macmillan, 1952.

Wright, Esmond. *The Fire of Liberty*. New York: St. Martin's, 1983.

Index

Adams, John, 31, 53, 60
Adams, Samuel, 60, 82
American(s)
    allies, 32, 53
    and Benedict Arnold, 17
    Continental army, 13–15
    peace commission, 32
    and Revolution, 46, 80
Antifederalists, 82–84
    Bill of Rights, 79, 85
Arnold, Benedict, 16–17
Articles of Confederation, 50–52
    and Congress, 55
    and Convention, 58, 65
    and new constitution, 62
    and William Paterson, 66

Barras, Comte de, 22, 24
Bedford, Gunning, 67
Bicameral legislature, 48–50, 62
Bill of Rights, 79, 83
Bonaparte, Napoleon, 87
Boone, Daniel (pioneer), 40
Brant, Joseph (Thayendanegea), 38
    See also Mohawks

Cayugas (Iroquis tribe), 36
    See also Indians
Clark, George, 42–43, 45–46
Clinton, Henry, 15–17, 20, 27
Committee
    of detail, 71, 72
    report, grand, 67–69

Committee (*continued*)
    style, arrangement, 74
    unfinished parts, 73–74
    of the whole, 63–64, 66
Congress, 50–52, 55, 57, 58, 64
    Benedict Arnold, 16–17
    and Constitution, 82, 83
    seats, lower house of, 69
    and the slave trade, 72
    taxing power of the, 74
    and the Virginia Plan, 62
Constitution, 75, 80
    Alexander Hamilton, 84
    Bill of Rights, 79, 85
    and Congress, 82, 83
    self government, 78, 87
    and slavery, 72, 83, 88
    writers, 48, 49, 50, 74
Continental Congress, 15, 31
    and Constitution, 78
    General Washington, 38
    and Henry Hamilton, 42
    and John Dickinson, 50
    and Loyalists, 36
    Northwest Ordinance, 87
Continental government, 50
Convention, 58–61, 63–75
    and Luther Martin, 80
    nonbinding changes, 82
    and slavery debate, 72
    and United States, 78

Cornwallis, Lord Charles
    Admiral de Grasse, 21
    Henry Clinton, 16, 17–20
    and Tarleton's camp, 29
    Thomas Graves, 24

Declaration of Independence,
    50, 65, 68
Dickinson, John, 50

Ellsworth, Oliver, 71

Federalists
    and Constitution, 79–80
    and James Wilson, 82
    and Mount Vernon, 84
    papers, 80, 81
Franklin, Benjamin, 31
    Convention, 59, 67, 77
    George Mason, 69, 70
    and James Wilson, 75

Gerry, Elbridge, 67, 77
    and Constitution, 80
    and mob rule, 70
Gibault, Father, 43
Gorham, Nathaniel, 71, 75
Government
    American, 47, 48
    continental, 50
    mixed, 49

Government (*continued*)
   national, 55
   and paper money, 57
   republican form of, 63
   self, 68, 78
   of the Six Nations, 36
   of United States, 51
Grand Committee, 67–69
Grasse, Admiral Comte de,
   19
   commander, 21–22
Graves, Thomas, 21–22, 24
Great Compromise debate, 69,
   70
Greene, General Nathanael, 15

Hamilton, Alexander, 27, 74
   George Washington, 68–
    69
   and "Publius", 80
   and Virginia Plan, 63
Hamilton, Henry, 40, 42
   George Clark, 43, 45–46
Hancock, John, 60
   Convention, 82
Heath, General William, 19
Henry, Patrick, 42, 60
   and Antifederalists, 83
   and Bill of Rights, 85
   and the Constitution, 80
   and James Monroe, 83, 84
   See also Mason, George

House of Delegates, 48, 55
House of Representatives
   choose a president, 74
   lower house, 62, 72
   Nathaniel Gorham, 75

Indian(s)
   and Congress, 54
   and fur trading, 53
   George Clark, 42, 43
   Iroquois tribes, 36, 38
   and the Revolution, 40
   rights of, 36
   and white society, 48
Iroquois
   Confederation, 36
   lands, 40
   settlements, 38

Jay, John, 31
   Convention, 60
   and publius, 80
Jefferson, Thomas, 60
Johnson, William, 74

King, Rufus, 74

Lafayette, Marquis de, 21–22
   and American army, 15
   and detachments, 17
   General Washington, 19
   and Rochambeau, 24

Laurens, Henry, 31, 32
Legislature(s), 87
    bicameral, 48–50, 62
    and Parliament, 31, 32
    state, 74
    unicameral Congress, 65
    See also Virginia Plan
Loyalists, 32, 36, 85
    and the peace treaty, 53
    religious minorities, 49
    and Senecas, 38

Madison, James, 67, 70, 74, 77
    and Congress, 55, 85
    Convention, 55, 57–75
    and the Federalists, 84
    and New Jersey Plan, 66
    and "Publius", 80
    special ratification, 73
Marshall, John, 84
Martin, Luther, 66, 80
Mason, George, 68, 69, 70, 72
    and Constitution, 74
    and Edmund Randolph, 75
    and Elbridge Gerry, 77
    and Patrick Henry, 83
    ratification issue, 73
Mifflin, Thomas, 51
Mohawks (Iroquois), 36, 38
Monroe, James
    and Antifederalists, 84
    See also Mason, George

Morris, Robert, 60, 67, 74
    and John Dickinson, 70

New Jersey Plan, 65
    See also Legislature
North, Lord Frederick, 31
Northwest Ordinance, 87

Oneidas (Iroquois tribe), 38
    See also Indian(s)
Onondagas (Iroquois tribe), 36
    See also Indian(s)

Parliament, 31, 32
    and the King, 79
Paterson, William, 65, 66

Randolph, Edmund, 61, 74, 75
    committee of detail, 71
    and the Federalists, 84
    See also Wilson, James
Revolution(s), 59, 60, 68, 85
    and Antifederalists, 79
    and battlegrounds, 13
    and the Indians, 40, 42
    and royal governors, 47
    and self government, 87
Rochambeau, General Comte
de
    French troops, 13–14
    Washington, 15–17, 21
Rutledge, John, 71

Senate
  equal vote proposal, 67
  representation, 68, 69
  seats awarded in, 64, 66
  seats in Congress, 69
  upper house, 48, 49, 62
  and the vice president, 74
Senecas (Iroquois tribe), 36
  and Loyalists, 38
  See also Indian(s)
Shays, Daniel, 70
  rebellion leader, 57
Steuben, Baron Von, 25
Sullivan, General John, 38

Tarleton, Colonel Banastre, 24
  Gloucester Point, 29
Thayendanegea (Mohawk), 38
  See also Brant, Joseph
The Six Nations, 36, 40
Tuscaroras (Iroquois), 38
  See also Indian(s)

Unicameral Congress, 65
  See also Legislature
United States, 32, 35, 46, 85
  and Constitution, 81
  Napoleon Bonaparte, 87
  and prewar debts, 53
  and Spanish Empire, 54
  Supreme Court, 84

Virginia
  constitution, 48, 49, 62
  and Convention, 64, 71
  House of Delegates, 55
  and James Madison, 62–63
  Plan, 61–65

Washington, General George, 20
  and Antifederalists, 84
  Charles Cornwallis, 29, 31
  and Convention, 59, 68
  and Federalists, 84
  and French Navy, 21, 24
  General Clinton, 15–16
  and George Mason, 72
  and James Madison, 55, 60
  John Sullivan, 38, 40
  and Nathaniel Gorham, 75
  and Robert Morris, 60
  and Rochambeau, 14, 17, 19
  and Valley Forge, 71
  See also Franklin, Benjamin
Wilson, James, 67, 70, 75
  at Convention, 67, 73
  committee of detail, 71
  and the Federalists, 82
  special ratification, 73

DATE DUE

MAY 1 3		
FEB 27 '90		

HIGHSMITH   #LO-45220